Contents

Step-by-step Data Governance Implementation Guide by Carlos Barroso

Step-by-step Data Governance Implementation Guide by Carlos Barroso

Data is everything and everything is data

This is the Step-by-step Data Governance Implementation Guide, the ultimate guide for data governance implementation in the organization. The content of this book is the result of several researches done to ensure the best approach, methodology and frameworks were combined to give the most powerful guidance for Data Governance implementation in any organization independently of their size, industry or location.

This book was brought to you with the intent of helping you setting up a data governance program in your organization, independently of which stage you may already be in. As such, whether you are just considering starting a data governance program in your organization, or you have an already implemented program, this book will surely give you good insight into how to take it to the next level.

The Data Governance Implementation Guide is a comprehensive and valuable resource for organizations looking to establish, improve, or optimize their data governance practices. With its thorough research and carefully curated content, this guide provides a clear and effective path to successful data governance implementation. The guide covers all aspects of data governance, including setting objectives, establishing governance council, involving key stakeholders, and defining policies and procedures. The information presented is adaptable to organizations of any size, industry, or location, making it an ideal resource for businesses seeking to take their data governance program to the next level. Whether you are just starting out or looking to enhance your existing data governance program, this guide offers valuable insights and guidance for your journey.

About the author:

With over 20 years of professional experience, having performed key roles in data related disciplines over the years, currently CIO at CoFusion Corporation, Carlos Barroso is a data enthusiastic with deep data experience and an advanced technology passionate. At the age of 10 he had built his first computer, and from there moved on to build several other gadgets, including motors, drones, and several robots. He is also a savvy programmer in C#, Python, and C++.

By the time you finish reading this book you will:

- ✓ Be able to build a business case and explain in detail what it will take to implement data governance in your organization

- ✓ Understand the in's and out's of data governance, frameworks, best practices, models, tools, and the steps needed to implement data governance in your organization

- ✓ Better understand how Data Governance can support and enhance digital transformation programs in your organization

- ✓ Provide an overview of data governance and its importance to your organization.

- ✓ Demonstrate how data governance definitely enhances the various IT services in your organization

Introduction

We produce quintillion bytes of data day-by-day. The velocity in which we create data is accelerating incrementally as we digitalize more and evolve the computing power.

Just over the last two years, we managed to produce around 90 percent of the data in the world, and it is estimated that we will keep doubling the amount of data being produced every 2 to 3 years for the next 5 years at least.

The increasing amount of data being produced will have a significant impact on many areas and industries in the future. Some of the areas that are likely to be impacted include:

- Healthcare: With the increase in data, healthcare organizations will be able to analyze larger and more complex data sets, which will help in the development of new treatments and personalized medicine.
- Finance: The financial sector will benefit from the increase in data as it will allow for more advanced data analysis and predictive modeling, which will lead to better risk management and improved investment strategies.

- Retail: Retail organizations will use data to better understand consumer behavior, preferences and buying patterns. This information can be used to create more personalized and targeted marketing strategies, improve customer experience and increase sales.

- Manufacturing: With the increase in data, manufacturing companies will be able to make more informed decisions, improve their supply chain processes, reduce costs and increase efficiency.

- Transportation: The transportation industry will use data to optimize routes, improve safety, reduce costs and reduce emissions.

These are just a few examples of the industries that will be impacted by the increase in data. In general, data will play a critical role in shaping the future and helping organizations make more informed decisions, increase efficiency and improve outcomes.

Why is Data Governance important for the company?

Data Governance is important for companies for several reasons:

- Improved Data Quality: Data Governance helps to ensure that the data being used by the company is accurate, complete, consistent and reliable. This leads to better decision-making and improved business outcomes.

- Compliance: Data Governance helps companies comply with various regulations, such as GDPR and HIPAA, which protect the privacy and security of personal data.

- Better Data Management: Data Governance provides a framework for managing data, which includes defining roles and responsibilities, establishing policies and procedures, and monitoring data usage. This leads to better data management, which is critical for companies in today's data-driven world.

- Better Collaboration: Data Governance helps to improve collaboration between different departments and stakeholders, which leads to better communication and decision-making.

- Increased Trust: Companies that have a strong Data Governance program build trust with their customers, stakeholders, and partners by demonstrating that they take data privacy and security seriously.

Data Governance is important for companies because it helps to ensure that data is used in an effective and efficient manner, while also protecting the privacy and security of personal data.

Data is becoming the most important asset for organizations to the extent that proper data handling will be crucial for many organizations to survive and stay competitive. Still, many are the organizations that remain uninformed on how to manage their data.

Data in our organizations is growing at explosive rates in both volume and velocity in which data is produced. On top of that, now, with more and more companies leveraging from new mediums and networks, like social media for instance, the strain on enterprise data management is just growing bigger and bigger. And even though the need for a data governance program is obvious, business buy-in remains a real barrier to achieve proper governance.

- Gather the requirements for your data governance program by interviewing key stakeholders and identifying prevalent, data-related pains. Understand how data is created, used, and curated through the enterprise to gain a high-level perspective of data requirements.

- Identify the organization's current state of data governance capability along with the target state, identify the gaps, then define solutions across a balance of planning and control activities to fill those gaps. Ensure business initiatives are woven into the mix.

- Create a comprehensive roadmap to prioritize initiatives and delineate responsibilities amongst data stewards, data owners, and members of the data governance steering committee.

- Gain complete buy-in from the business and IT stakeholders to move forward with the implementation of data governance. Communicate initiatives to end users and executives to reduce resistance, as not everyone reacts positively to change.

The rise of Data Economy

Organizations can be placed in one of four different categories based on how they use their data:

Dataphobes   Data Mixers   Data Builders   Datavores

Step-by-step Data Governance Implementation Guide by Carlos Barroso

Data is quickly becoming the most value asset of the company, and the **more it is used, the higher its value gets**. In todays, and predicted future, data will have such value that businesses won't be able to stay competitive without managing their data properly.

Getting to the basics of Data Governance

The DAMA Dictionary of Data Management defines **Data Governance** as 'The exercise of authority, control and shared decision making (planning, monitoring and enforcement) over the management of data assets.' DAMA has identified 10 major functions of Data Management in the DAMA-DMBOK (Data Management Body of Knowledge).

Choosing the best Data Governance model for your organization

Data Governance models traditionally entail key elements which usually cover policies, benefits, risks, and best practices.

So, what is a Data Governance model, you may ask. A data governance model is a framework that takes into consideration the following aspects of data: 1) data generation, 2) data storage, 3) maintenance, and 4) data disposal processes and systems. There are numerous data governance models out there, rather than just a single model being applied by every company. One of the key variations of these Models comes from the relation with whom the data is being collected and analyzed. According to NTT DATA, there are four common data governance models:

1) Decentralized with single business units

2) Decentralized with multiple business units

3) Centralized in all aspects

4) Centralized with de-centralized execution

Historically speaking, centralized systems for the creation of data hubs have been around for some time now. Master Data Management and enterprise data warehouses are some examples of these centralized systems.

A highly centralized approach depends on a small group of vastly knowledgeable data experts who should be extremely familiar with well-defined processes and best practices.

A data governance model outlines the elementary structure of responsibility for master data management, while data governance policies define the people, processes, and technologies for managing the data.

So, which model to choose from?

De-centralized Execution – Single Business Unit

This data governance model is considered mostly by individual business users who wish, or need, to preserve their own master data. This is a model where data producers and data consumers are one and the same.

- Best for small organizations, such as a single plant or single company

- Offers simpler data maintenance

- Requires a lot of agility in order to set up master data

- No shared master data with other business units

- Delivers a shorter life span for master data

Organization size and simplicity are two of the key drivers for this particular model. Data inconsistencies is one of the key problems with this model, and one of the reasons for not recommending it for bigger corporations. However, there are ways to minimize impact and ensure this model works effectively:

- Clearly define data ownership and limit this to a handful of experts within the organization

Step-by-step Data Governance Implementation Guide by Carlos Barroso

- Ensure clear documentation of how each field is to be populated and the meaning of each value for each field

- If budget permits, automated tools can control the consistency of data

- Set up controls and audits to quickly fix any inconsistencies

- Limit the role of data governance organization to building processes and procedures and performing periodic data audits

De-Centralized Execution – Multiple Business Units

This data governance model is mostly considered when particular business users wish, or must, maintain their own master data. In this setup, we would then have multiple business units working with shared customers, materials and vendors.

Users, benefits and caveats:

- Best for small and medium organizations, with multiple plants and/or multiple companies involved

- Offers simpler data maintenance

- Requires a lot of agility in order to set up master data

- Allows for shared master data with other business units

- Delivers a shorter life span for master data

This is also a quite simple model and can enable quicker master data setup. However, as with the previous model, it can also result in inconsistent data with a far-reaching impact when multiple parties are involved. Some examples of the impact can be inconsistency and inaccuracy of key data, which ultimately may affect reporting.

To make it work more effective, the following can be implemented:

Step-by-step Data Governance Implementation Guide by Carlos Barroso

- Leverage automated tools that can ensure the consistency of data – independent of who creates the master data

- Limit the number of fields that are maintained and let the rest of the fields be derived based on various customized profiles

- Ensure clear documentation of how each field is to be populated and what is the meaning of each value for each field

- Set up controls and audits to quickly fix any inconsistencies

- Identify controlled fields that have an impact across departments and business units, then enforce strict controls on who maintains these and clearly define what each field means

- The role of the data governance organization should not be limited to building processes and procedures and performing periodic data audits, but should also include owning the automated tools and keeping them tuned to business requirements

Centralized Governance – Single or Multiple Business Units

Centralized models tend to have some key advantages especially when considering the right model for bigger organizations where various people need to produce and consume data. In this particular model, one central organization owns the master data and works on it based on the needs of the consumers of the data.

Users, benefits and caveats:

- Best for large and medium organizations with multiple plants, and/or multiple companies

- Brings complex data requirements

- Supports a longer life span for master data, with a longer product life cycle and long term relationships with customers and vendors

- Involves a lot of legal implications and must be kept up to date based on extrinsic factors like government regulations

- Allows for shared master data with other business units

- Entails a larger system landscape and requires master data to be distributed to various systems

This data governance model can ensure a high level of control of master data, but it is often characterized by delays in setting up master data and requires a formal and larger data governance organization. As well, in this model there is high probability that the master data created is consistent and introduction of changes and process improvements is quicker because there are a limited number of users setting up master data. In order to improve the model, organizations should:

- Build automated processes to provide transparency and visibility to the process of master data maintenance

- Establish KPIs for different master data requests and ensure the size of the data governance organization scales based on the requirements

- Confirm effective communication takes place between the business and master data team to ensure that master data rules are tuned to changes in the business and products

- The role of the data governance organization should not be limited to processes and procedures but should also include maintenance of master data, including process adjustments to meet business needs

Centralized Data Governance & Decentralized Execution

Similar to the previous model, but this time, more characterized by a centralized governance body which defines the framework of controls and standards which individual businesses creating their individual parts of master data should conform to.

Users, benefits and caveats:

- Best for large and medium organizations with multiple plant and/or multiple companies

- Brings complex data requirements but requires agility in the creation of master data

- Supports a longer life span for master data, with a longer product life cycle and long term relationships with customers and vendors

Step-by-step Data Governance Implementation Guide by Carlos Barroso

- Involves a lot of legal implications and must be kept up to date based on extrinsic factors like government regulations

- Allows for shared master data with other business units

- Entails a larger system landscape and requires master data to be distributed to various systems

Agility, scalability, security and more are some of the key benefits of this model. Nonetheless, it is important that the organizations safeguard the proper controls and ensure they are in place and being applied wherever needed. A key aspect of this model is the shared responsibility between the data governance organization and the business.

To effectively leverage this model organizations must:

- Identify controlled fields that have an impact across departments and business units, and then assign ownership to centralize maintenance

- Build automated tools to avoid de-duplication at the source

- Ensure a central organization mediate between various departments and business units when there is a conflict

- Automate the request process and leverage automated tools to help local businesses consistently manage data

- Set up controls and audits to quickly fix any inconsistencies

- The role of the data governance organization should not be limited to processes and procedures but should also include maintenance of part of the master data, including making process adjustments to meet business needs. Here, the master data team also plays a mentoring role to the business in order to ensure consistency

Any of these four data governance models can be implemented in any organization, but one may work better for a particular company than another one, due to different constraints, like company size, data governance goals, vision, and so on.

Whichever model you choose for your organization, the following chapters will tell you how to implement Data Governance in your organization. The rules and steps applying for whichever model are similar, and the recommendation is always to start small and grow bigger. This way, there is always opportunity for improvement of each step while minimizing subsequent implementation risks.

Become a *Datavore* and leave the competition behind

If you really want to stay ahead of the competition, we recommend that you become a Datavore. Leveraging from Data with a good data governance program in place, and you will then be powered by an enabling framework of decision rights and accountabilities for information-related processes.

You will have powerful Working models that that will give guidance of who can take particular actions. What actions those are, and what and when particular information should be accessed and for what purpose.

This will also lead to a True business-IT collaboration that will further lead to assurance, reliability and confidence in decision making, leading to visible innovation and evolution.

Data governance will give you:

- An enabling framework of decision rights and accountabilities for information-related processes
- Working models that that give guidance of who can take what actions with what information, when, and using what methods
- True business-IT collaboration that will lead to assurance, reliability and confidence in decision making, leading to visible innovation and evolution

Data governance brings sense to an organization's data. It brings assurance of better decision making thanks to the trust and understanding of company's data it brings to the organization, thus accelerating digital transformation across the enterprise.

1

Get the right data, to the right people, at the right time, and you will see huge change. Data governance helps protect a company's most important assets: knowledge and data.

Key benefits of Data Governance:

- Improved decision making
- Improved risk mitigation
- Improved transformation
- Improved performance
- Cost reduction
- Increased sales

Data governance empowers the organization with the right framework and tools to take full advantage of their BI, big data, CRM, and ERP projects and technologies. Projects that are data-intensive must have some form of data governance to help guiding and aligning towards realistic expectations.

Data Governance can have a positive impact on your career as well by providing the following benefits:

- Improved Skill Set: Understanding Data Governance principles and practices can enhance your technical and analytical skills, making you more valuable to potential employers.

- Career Advancement: As organizations place more emphasis on managing data effectively, having a background in Data Governance can increase your opportunities for advancement within your company or in finding new job opportunities.

- Increased Demand for Data Governance Expertise: With the growing importance of data in organizations, the demand for individuals with Data Governance expertise is increasing. This can lead to higher salaries and greater job security.

Step-by-step Data Governance Implementation Guide by Carlos Barroso

- Better Understanding of Data Management: By learning about Data Governance, you will gain a better understanding of the importance of data management, which can help you make informed decisions about the collection, use, and protection of data in your personal and professional life.

- Compliance with Data Protection Regulations: Understanding Data Governance can help you comply with data protection regulations, such as GDPR, which can protect your personal information and ensure that you are following best practices in your career.

As such, Data Governance can bring a range of benefits to your career by improving your skills, advancing your career opportunities, and ensuring compliance with data protection regulations.

Common mistakes made during the implementation of a data governance project.

- Lack of Executive Support: Without strong support from upper management, a data governance implementation project can struggle to gain traction and achieve its goals.

- Inadequate Resource Allocation: A lack of resources, including personnel, budget, and technology, can undermine the success of a data governance implementation project.

- Poor Communication: Inadequate communication between stakeholders can lead to misunderstandings, missed deadlines, and misaligned expectations.

- Complex Technical Challenges: The technical aspects of data governance can be complex, requiring specialized skills and expertise. This can create challenges in the implementation of data governance solutions and processes.

- Resistance to Change: Change can be difficult for organizations, and a data governance implementation project can encounter resistance from employees who are used to working with existing systems and processes.

- Insufficient Data Quality: Data governance solutions can only be effective if the data being managed is of high quality. Poor data quality can impact the implementation of data governance and hinder its success.

- Unclear Responsibilities: If roles and responsibilities are not clearly defined and communicated, it can lead to confusion, inefficiency, and misunderstandings in the implementation of data governance.

Avoiding these pitfalls requires careful planning, strong leadership, adequate resources, effective communication, and a commitment to change and continuous improvement.

A methodology that fulfills actual needs

A Data Governance Framework is important because it provides a structure for defining, communicating, and implementing data governance policies and processes within an organization. The framework ensures that data is managed in a consistent, efficient, and effective manner, enabling the organization to effectively utilize its data assets to support business objectives. The framework also provides a means of ensuring that data privacy, security, and regulatory compliance requirements are met.

Having a Data Governance Framework in place helps organizations improve the quality of their data, which in turn leads to better decision making, increased operational efficiency, and enhanced customer satisfaction. Additionally, the framework provides a common understanding of data management practices and helps to ensure that everyone in the organization is working towards the same goals. The framework can also facilitate communication and collaboration between departments, improving cross-functional data management processes.

A Data Governance Framework is critical for ensuring that an organization can effectively manage its data assets and realize the full value of its data.

Data governance can be thought of as the engine that enables your data to be transformed into the power needed to drive your organization up the data value chain. Fueled by the data, information, and needs of the business, data governance puts into the spotlight MDM, data quality, and data architecture and makes sure that these are both in alignment as well as in motion. The deliverables are the power out of the data governance engine, creating motion up the value chain.

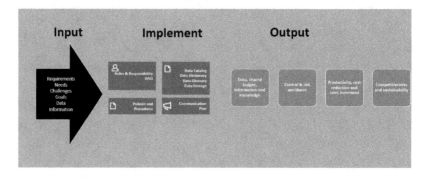

The 3phase approach to Data Governance

The 3phase approach to Data Governance is a framework that organizations can use to implement a comprehensive Data Governance program. The three phases are as follows:

Step-by-step Data Governance Implementation Guide by Carlos Barroso

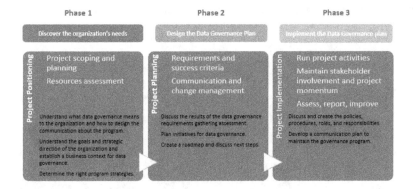

Phase 1 — Discover the organization's needs

Project Positioning
- Project scoping and planning
- Resources assessment

Understand what data governance means to the organization and how to design the communication about the program.

Understand the goals and strategic direction of the organization and establish a business context for data governance.

Determine the right program strategies.

Phase 2 — Design the Data Governance Plan

Project Planning
- Requirements and success criteria
- Communication and change management

Discuss the results of the data governance requirements gathering assessment.

Plan initiatives for data governance.

Create a roadmap and discuss next steps.

Phase 3 — Implement the Data Governance plan

Project Implementation
- Run project activities
- Maintain stakeholder involvement and project momentum
- Assess, report, improve

Discuss and create the policies, procedures, roles, and responsibilities.

Develop a communication plan to maintain the governance program.

The first phase of a data governance approach is discovery, where the organization's needs and current state of data management are assessed. This phase involves identifying key stakeholders, data assets, and any existing data policies, standards, and processes. The goal of this phase is to understand the organization's data landscape, including its strengths, weaknesses, and potential risks, in order to determine what data governance initiatives should be prioritized.

The second phase of a data governance approach is design, where the data governance plan is created. This phase involves defining the roles, responsibilities, and processes necessary to effectively manage data across the organization. The data governance plan should include guidelines for data management, data quality, data security, and data privacy, as well as procedures for data integration, data warehousing, and data analysis. The goal of this phase is to create a comprehensive plan that can be used to guide the implementation and ongoing management of data governance initiatives.

The third phase of a data governance approach is implementation, where the data governance plan is put into action. This phase involves establishing the data governance program, including the creation of governance committees, the appointment of data stewards, and the development of data management tools and technologies. The goal of this phase is to establish the necessary structures and systems to ensure the effective management of data within the organization. This may include establishing data quality metrics, data security protocols, and data privacy standards, as well as designing data

Step-by-step Data Governance Implementation Guide by Carlos Barroso

management workflows and data governance dashboards to monitor progress and ensure ongoing compliance.

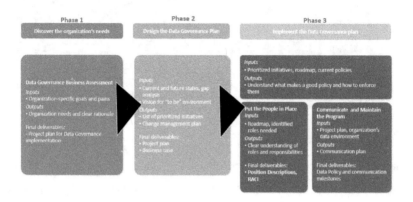

Using a three-phase data governance framework can bring several benefits to the company. Some of the key advantages include:

- Clarity and structure: The three-phase approach provides a clear roadmap for data governance implementation, ensuring that all critical steps are taken in a structured and organized manner.

- Improved data quality: By establishing data quality metrics and protocols, the implementation of a data governance framework can help to improve the accuracy, completeness, and consistency of the data in your company, leading to better decision-making and improved business outcomes.

- Enhanced data security: Data security is a key component of data governance, and the three-phase approach provides a structured way to ensure that your company's data is secure and protected against unauthorized access, theft, or misuse.

Step-by-step Data Governance Implementation Guide by Carlos Barroso

- Improved data privacy: With the increasing importance of data privacy regulations, implementing a data governance framework can help your company ensure that it is in compliance with relevant regulations and that the privacy of your customers and clients is protected.

- Better data management: By establishing clear roles and responsibilities for data management, as well as workflows and tools for data management, the three-phase approach can help your company to improve its data management processes, reducing the risk of data errors or duplication and improving data consistency.

- Overall, using a three-phase data governance framework can provide a solid foundation for managing your company's data, ensuring that it is of high quality, secure, and in compliance with regulations, and that your company is well-equipped to make informed decisions based on the data it holds.

Tools to help you implement Data Governance

Data governance tools are important for implementing data governance as they provide an efficient and effective way to manage, monitor, and enforce data-related policies and standards across an organization. These tools can help automate manual processes, ensure data quality, improve data security and privacy, promote collaboration among stakeholders, and provide a centralized platform for managing data-related activities. By using data governance tools, companies can improve the overall quality, accuracy, and consistency of their data and make better data-driven decisions.

We have covered the introduction to Data Governance and its implementation in the organization. Next, we will cover the step-by-step on how to implement Data Governance in your organization using blueprints which will help to adopt a structured and iterative strategy in implementing Data Governance. Following the 3 phases outlined in this book will support you in designing the right strategies and building a plan that will enable data users to:

- ✓ Have access to correct and trustworthy data.

- ✓ Have access to the right data thus improving the reporting, analytical, and operational data to day business.

- ✓ Have assurance of data security and compliance.

Data Governance is the set of processes and policies that ensure the effective and efficient management of an organization's data assets. It is important because it helps organizations ensure the accuracy, reliability, and availability of their data, while also ensuring that they comply with legal and regulatory requirements and protect sensitive information. A well-implemented Data Governance program can improve decision-making, reduce operational risks, increase efficiency, and enhance the overall value of an organization's data assets. Having a solid and proven framework will give you half of the tools you need to successfully implement Data Governance in your organization. However, the remaining tools which we will discuss in the next chapters will give you full power into discovering your organization's needs, planning for the Data Governance implementation, sell it to the key stakeholders and sponsors, and ultimately implement Data Governance across the organization with 100% success. As such, let's then discuss the first phase of the framework and get a better understanding of what are your organization's actual needs.

Phase 1: Discover the organization's needs

It is time to start the analyze and preparation for Data Governance in the organization, and to make the journey as smooth as possible, we will approach it in stages or phases if you prefer. Below we have the outline of the steps needed to complete phase 1 and have the discovery of the organizations needs done.

Step-by-step Data Governance Implementation Guide by Carlos Barroso

Phase 1 Results & Insights:

- A scoped and planned business case for the data governance program.

- Stakeholder buy-in and a clear understanding of the value of data within the context of your organization.

- An approved and launched data governance project.

Step 1 - Discover the organization's needs

The first step of data governance is the discovery of the organization's needs. This step involves conducting a comprehensive analysis of the organization's data assets, processes, and stakeholders to understand how data is used, managed, and protected. The goal of this step is to identify areas where data governance can improve the organization's data management practices and support its business objectives.

- Data Inventory: An inventory of all the data assets in the organization is created. This includes data sources, databases, data warehouses, and other data repositories. The inventory should provide a comprehensive understanding of the data types, formats, structures, and ownership of the data assets.

- Data Process Mapping: The data processes and workflows in the organization are mapped out to understand how data is acquired, processed, stored, and used. This includes processes such as data entry, data validation, data storage, and data retrieval.

- Stakeholder Analysis: The stakeholders who are involved in the data processes and who have a stake in the organization's data assets are identified. This includes employees, customers, partners, and regulatory bodies.

- Business Requirements: The business requirements and objectives of the organization are analyzed to understand how data is used to support business goals. This includes understanding the data requirements of different departments, such as marketing, finance, and operations.

By conducting a thorough discovery of the organization's needs, the first step of data governance sets the foundation for creating a robust data governance framework that can improve data management practices and support the organization's business objectives.

Organizations traditionally start considering data governance when they feel the data quality is poor, or they fear possible consequences as a result of misuse of data, be it personal or simply classified.

As a Business:

- There is uncertainty as to whether the data is complying with laws and regulations.
- The business has trouble executing its main business processes due to bad data.
- Employees get different answers from what are supposed to be the same data sets.
- There is a genuine inability to make good business decisions because the data is of such low quality.
- The business is experiencing severe dissatisfaction from customers, partners, and suppliers alike due to bad data and it is eroding our reputation.
- The business is leaking money as a result of duplicate mailings, time wasted finding new customer information, etc.

As CIO and IT department:

- The business continues to complain to IT that the organizational **data is inadequate** for its operations.
- CIO and IT department feel that they need to step in to alleviate pains caused from bad data.
- IT has spent **countless person-hours sifting** through data to resolve issues, wasting time and money.

- The business insists that IT is responsible and IT takes measures to rectify the issue, but clean-up efforts are futile: regardless of the tools we employ, the data gets dirty again, almost immediately.

Four drivers of Data Governance

- Compliance: Compliance with regulatory requirements and industry standards is one of the key drivers of data governance. Organizations need to ensure that their data management practices comply with laws and regulations, such as the General Data Protection Regulation (GDPR), the Health Insurance Portability and Accountability Act (HIPAA), and the Sarbanes-Oxley Act (SOX).

- Risk Management or Security: Data governance helps organizations manage the risks associated with data, such as the risk of data breaches, data loss, or data inaccuracies. By implementing data governance policies and procedures, organizations can reduce the likelihood of these risks and minimize their impact.

- Data Quality or Data Trust: Data quality is a critical factor in the success of data-driven initiatives. Poor data quality can lead to incorrect business decisions, decreased operational efficiency, and decreased customer satisfaction. Data governance helps organizations ensure that their data is accurate, complete, and consistent, which in turn supports the quality of data-driven decision making.

- Business Agility or Data Availability: Data governance can also help organizations become more agile by enabling them to quickly and effectively respond to changes in the business environment. This can be achieved through the implementation of efficient data management processes and the use of technology to support data governance practices. By improving the quality and reliability of their data, organizations can make informed decisions more quickly and respond to changing business needs more effectively.

These four drivers of data governance are interrelated and must be considered together to ensure that data governance is effective and sustainable. A well-designed data governance program will address all four drivers and provide a foundation for the successful management and use of data within an organization.

Pressure for Data Governance adoption

Extensive changes to the business environment, like Big Data, Rapid Technological Evolution, security, competitive pressures, and social media, have placed pressure on the business to adopt data governance.

As companies continue to grow and generate progressively large volumes of data, their ability to staff and manage this digital universe continues to fall behind the perpetual increase of data being stored. It is becoming costly and inefficient for a company to find specific information in their cosmos of unstructured data.

With new technological advancements being introduced to the market every day, many companies pursue these technological trends in an attempt to increase efficiency in their business practices. However, with these technologies (mobile devices, cloud computing, SaaS models, and on-demand computing) comes several new ways to store information and subsequently organize data. Organizing this data seems to be an afterthought for most companies. They would benefit from developing a strategy for these specific issues ahead of time.

Many industries are disposed to cyber attacks (financial, medical, government, etc.). The success of cyber attacks is generally due to the overload of new technology mixing with older systems without proper integration and governance. Instilling security policies is a good first step; however, it is extremely hard to maintain without proper data governance.

Step-by-step Data Governance Implementation Guide by Carlos Barroso

It is a clear competitive advantage for companies to hold a proactive business model. Effective data governance is an organizational strategy that is a key element in holding this competitive advantage over those companies that have yet to invest in their long-term strategies.

In the era of social media, the pressure for transparency is greater than ever before. Customers will not choose to buy from non-transparent companies.

Construct your Business Data Glossary to identify the crucial business data that will be subject to governance.

Kick-start your data governance program by understanding why the business needs it – the fuel for the Data Governance engine.

Data governance and data empowerment is ultimately meant to support the goals and objectives of the organization. If you don't know why business units need data governance, the project will be focused on improving data quality without a larger purpose. This will not only be unsustainable but also a waste of time for the organization.

Before trying to force data governance into an unreceptive environment, you have to make sure that the business is on board, naturally thinking in this manner, and actively evangelizing the ability of proper data governance to enable shared insight.

The following activities will bring you through the most important steps of the data governance program:

- Work with the business to unite under WHY the business needs data governance and help the business understand these reasons.

Step-by-step Data Governance Implementation Guide by Carlos Barroso

- Collaborate with the business to figure out HOW data governance will help drive the long-term goals and strategies of the organization to get the right information to the right people at the right time.

- Combine your ideas and efforts to establish WHAT you can do to accomplish the success of data governance implementation for the business

In an ideal world, you would have all the resources that you need to govern all of the organization's data. This is rarely the case, if ever. Instead, target a realistic data scope to govern that will fit within your resourcing. To do this, figure out which is the most important data to the business.

These activities will help you accomplish the following outcomes:

1. Identify the key data that should fall under the scope of the data governance program, based on targeted input from the business units that need improved data usability and access.

2. Generate a data flow diagram that will document the relationships between essential aspects of key organizational data such as where it is stored, who uses it, and for what purpose.

3. Create a Business Data Glossary (BDG) to document the data that will be governed and their essential attributes such as ownership and uses.

4. Identify purposeful, business-driven pilot program initiatives that will help you start the data governance program, show quick value of the program, and popularize/socialize the program to other business units that may be skeptical of the value.

Step-by-step Data Governance Implementation Guide by Carlos Barroso

Okay, it's time to put into practice what we've learned so far and to do so, use the roundtable discussion approach, as well as deep-dive interviews and conduct a risk/value assessment. Those should give you a good kick-start with better understanding your organization and the need for Data Governance.

Understanding Data Movement

Data isn't static; it moves in and out of systems and is used for various purposes by multiple user groups Identifying the location of data can be difficult because it is frequently in transit and rarely stays in a single location. It's worth investing the time to develop a data flow diagram due to several advantages. By charting the movement of data, you can gain clarity on where the data is located and how it travels through the enterprise systems. Having a visual representation of the movement and utilization of data helps to comprehend who is utilizing it and how it is being altered at various stages. Additionally, a data flow diagram will enable you to see how data is utilized in diverse scenarios.

The creation of a data flow diagram is essential to commence the collection of requirements: By determining the location of data, you can quickly determine which business stakeholders to consult. It will facilitate the identification of possibilities for data cleansing and management: for example, it will help you determine where you need data owners and stewards, and provide a systematic approach to assign these roles. Moreover, it will provide insight into the security needs and compliance considerations.

A data flow diagram can bring value to an organization by enabling them to adopt a proactive approach to data governance. By understanding the entry points, you can save time and easily identify potential data issues.

Develop a Business Data Glossary to optimize comprehension of the key data within the organization.

The significance of having a thorough Business Data Glossary is that it governs business terms, their meanings, and relevant information, including who is responsible for the data and how it should be used

Step-by-step Data Governance Implementation Guide by Carlos Barroso

and when. This can improve the precision of reports as there are no conflicting definitions of data between business units. It also provides improved access to business term knowledge. On top of that, it aligns the business terminology with the technology and organizational assets, allowing individuals who interact with the data to easily recognize the applications, processes, and stewardship related to it. Finally, it boosts the accuracy and speed of searches for organizational data definitions and attributes, providing better data accessibility.

Having a Business Data Glossary does not guarantee that all of the organization's data challenges will be solved, but when paired with effective active governance, it can contribute to improved data access and accuracy.

Elements of a Business Data Glossary

1. Data element name

2. Definition

3. Abbreviations and acronyms

4. Source system

5. Source detail

6. Possible values

7. Data steward

8. Data sensitivity

9. Usage of the data

By utilizing the data flow model to populate the organization's Business Data Glossary, you can ensure that the vital data that is critical to key business systems and users is properly assigned and defined. This also establishes guidelines that facilitate proper data management and quality, which will be upheld by the designated data owners.

Step-by-step Data Governance Implementation Guide by Carlos Barroso

Identify the 3 key drivers for 2-3 business units to prime the data governance engine with pilot projects

Before launching any new data governance efforts, it is crucial to comprehend the present state of the organization's data governance program. This entails understanding the policies, procedures, and processes currently in place. This information can then be used to determine any shortcomings or opportunities for improvement. Based on the evaluation of the current data governance program, achievable goals and objectives can be established for the new initiatives. This helps to prevent setting unrealistic expectations or investing in areas that yield limited results.

By comprehending the status of the data governance program, the organization can make informed choices about allocating its resources and investments to improve efficiency and effectiveness. For instance, if the organization already has a well-established data classification system, it may not be necessary to make substantial investments in this area. The evaluation of the current data governance program can aid in aligning data governance efforts with the organization's overall business objectives. This helps to ensure that the data governance program is meeting the needs of the business, not just the IT department. Therefore, assessing the maturity of the existing data governance program is crucial for informed decision-making in implementing data governance in the organization, increasing efficiency, establishing achievable goals, and aligning data governance efforts with business objectives.

A maturity assessment typically covers several areas of data governance, including:

- Data management: This includes evaluating how data is stored, managed, and protected across the organization.
- Data quality: This involves assessing the quality of the data, including its accuracy, completeness, and consistency.
- Data security: This involves evaluating the security of the data and determining whether appropriate measures are in place to protect sensitive information.
- Data privacy: This involves assessing the organization's compliance with data privacy regulations, such as GDPR or CCPA, and determining whether the necessary measures are in place to protect personal data.

Step-by-step Data Governance Implementation Guide by Carlos Barroso

- Data governance structure: This involves evaluating the organization's data governance framework, including roles, responsibilities, and decision-making processes.

The results of a maturity assessment can be used to create a roadmap for data governance improvement and to prioritize areas for investment. The assessment can also help organizations understand their current level of data governance maturity, identify gaps and inefficiencies, and make informed decisions about future investments in data governance technology and practices.

The Data Management Framework of DMBOK2 has data governance as its core component

DAMA DMBOK stands for Data Management Body of Knowledge, which is a framework developed by the Data Management Association (DAMA) to provide a comprehensive guide to the field of data management. DMBOK outlines best practices, processes, and techniques for managing data as an asset in organizations. It provides a standardized approach to data management and covers topics such as data governance, data architecture, data quality, data integration, metadata management, and more. The goal of DMBOK is to help organizations effectively manage their data assets and to promote the growth and development of the data management profession.

A data governance program typically consists of several key components, including:

- Data Policy: A clear set of rules, principles, and guidelines that govern how data is collected, managed, used, and protected within an organization.

- Data Stewardship: The responsibility assigned to individuals or groups to manage the data assets of an organization. This includes defining data policies, ensuring data quality, and ensuring compliance with regulations and standards.

Step-by-step Data Governance Implementation Guide by Carlos Barroso

- Data Architecture: The design and structure of the systems, processes, and technologies that support the management of data assets. This includes data models, data dictionaries, metadata, and data flows.

- Data Management Processes: The specific processes and procedures used to manage data assets, such as data quality, data privacy, and data security.

- Data Metrics and Monitoring: The measurement and tracking of data quality, usage, and performance, used to monitor the effectiveness of the data governance program and identify areas for improvement.

- Data Governance Council: A group of stakeholders who provide strategic direction and oversee the implementation of the data governance program. This may include representatives from various business units, IT, and compliance teams.

- Data Technology and Tools: The technology and tools used to support the data governance program, such as data management platforms, data discovery tools, and metadata management tools.

Having these components in place can help organizations effectively manage their data assets, improve data quality and accuracy, and ensure compliance with regulations and standards.

Going deeper

Before assessing your organization's current state of data governance, take a minute to understand the CMMI program. To assess data governance functions, we look at the Capability Maturity Model Integration (CMMI) program for rating governance capabilities in each of the function areas.

The Capability Maturity Model (CMM) is a framework for evaluating and improving processes of an organization. The CMM provides a systematic approach to assessing the maturity of an organization's processes and helps organizations identify areas for improvement. The model is based on five levels of maturity, ranging from ad hoc and chaotic processes at Level 1 to a highly-structured, quantitatively managed process at Level 5. The model provides guidance on best practices and processes that organizations can implement at each level to improve their capability. The CMM is widely used by software development organizations and has been integrated into a number of other methodologies, including the Capability Maturity Model Integration (CMMI).

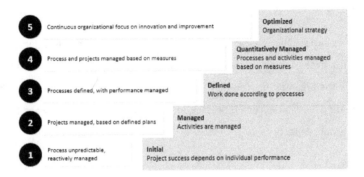

By increasing your data governance maturity, the organization will move from chaotic to predictive.

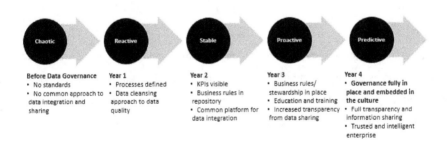

Structure the Data Governance implementation Program

The next step in establishing a data governance program is to organize its implementation. This involves setting clear objectives, determining the scope, and defining the framework for implementation.

Step-by-step Data Governance Implementation Guide by Carlos Barroso

The initial step is to outline the goals of the data governance program. This encompasses defining its purpose, such as enhancing data quality, increasing data security, or complying with data privacy regulations.

The coverage of the data governance program must then be established. This involves specifying the areas within the organization that will be impacted by the program and the stakeholders who will be involved. It's crucial to include critical stakeholders, such as business units, IT departments, and data management teams, in this process to ensure that their needs and views are considered.

Once the objectives and scope are established, the framework for implementing data governance must be established. This involves outlining the structure and procedures that will be utilized to enforce data governance within the organization. This may include defining the duties and responsibilities of key stakeholders, creating decision-making processes, and specifying the technology and tools that will support data governance practices.

In addition, it's essential to set metrics and KPIs to measure the success of the data governance program. This will help track progress and maintain alignment with the organization's goals and objectives.

By organizing the data governance implementation program, organizations can ensure that data governance becomes a seamless part of the organization's operations and decision-making processes. This will guarantee consistent and effective implementation of data governance practices and the sustainability of the program in the long run.

A data governance initiative must involve more than just IT - it requires the active participation of the business as they are the ones who hold ownership over the data. The collaboration between IT and the business is crucial in this process, however, it is essential that the business takes ownership of the governance program as a whole.

Step-by-step Data Governance Implementation Guide by Carlos Barroso

- The objective of data governance is to establish agreed-upon definitions and business rules that cater to the specific needs of different stakeholder groups, while also creating a centralized source of authoritative enterprise data. When changes to data processes and definitions are necessary, data governance serves as the final arbiter.

- Data governance ensures that the right individuals, who are responsible for handling data, are involved in decisions regarding data usage, quality, business processes, and change implementation.

- The purpose of a data governance program is to bring together individuals across different lines of business within the organization who have a vested interest in maintaining current data systems and processes, while also recognizing the importance of organization-wide policies for maintaining consistent data.

To launch a successful data governance program, it is crucial to have the right initiatives in place for people, processes, and technologies related to your data. The involvement of all relevant stakeholders is crucial in this process.

Creating a project charter that outlines the fundamentals of project management can help secure the support of the business. One of the primary steps in launching data governance effectively is to gain the approval of senior executives. The project charter can be used to communicate the significance of data governance to executives and secure the necessary backing to initiate a data governance project.

Define the vision, mission, objective, and targets of the data governance program.

Having a clear and concise vision statement is crucial in effectively communicating the importance of data governance within your organization. This vision statement should align the business and IT understanding of the long-term goals and objectives of the data governance program. To craft an impactful vision statement, consider using these starting ideas:

Step-by-step Data Governance Implementation Guide by Carlos Barroso

- Highlight the criticality of data governance in the organization
- Establish a unified understanding of the 3–5-year plan
- Emphasize the objectives of the data governance program.

Some starting points include:

- Business-IT collaboration

- The organization is dedicated to creating a data governance program with shared responsibilities between the business and IT that will foster a standard approach to *identifying, using,* and *understanding* data across all areas.

- The organization is dedicated to creating a data governance program that consists of an enabling structure that helps the organization get the *right information*, to the *right people*, at the *right time*.

- To accurately interpret and analyze data from different systems with confidence that data attributes and definitions conform to enterprise standards established through data governance policies and procedures.

Having a clear mission statement for your data governance program is important as it outlines the purpose and objectives of the program. It highlights what the program aims to achieve, the benefits it will bring to the business, and how it will enhance the organization's strategic utilization of its data.

Use these starting ideas as a foundation to create your own mission statement for your data governance program. Some initial examples are:

- Create a comprehensive enterprise data governance framework to enhance services, planning, and policy implementation throughout the organization.
- Determine the authority for creating policies and procedures that impact business data.
- Align data initiatives with the organization's strategies to promote consistent goals.

- Efficiently manage and preserve data resources while maintaining their integrity, reliability, availability, and compliance with regulations.
- Reduce the risk of misusing data through effective implementation of policies and procedures.
- Enhance compliance with regulatory requirements and improve the overall security of organizational data.
- Establish a lasting structure to ensure ongoing adherence to data governance.
- Transform data into valuable information that supports the organization's objectives.

Avoid common challenges and implement metrics during the launch of the data governance program.

Reducing the challenges faced during the launch of a data governance program can be achieved by determining key metrics for your organization and implementing them. While assigning data steward roles is important, it does not address the difficulties inherent in launching a data governance initiative.

The absence of challenge score assesses the presence of challenges within an organization that has implemented a data governance program.

- Determining key metrics to measure data governance success.
- Lack of consistent data definitions and data structures across lines of business.
- Staff resistance to following new governance guidelines and processes.
- Lack of staff resources willing to take accountability for data governance processes.
- High regulatory standards of some data sets.

The above challenges were prevalent among 79% of organizations when launching their data governance programs. Every organization's goals for data governance are unique, so the metrics used to measure its success should be tailored to its specific business objectives and desired outcomes.

There are two broad groupings of governance metrics that can be used:

Quantitative – those metrics that measure hard benefits such as resource allocation savings or reduction in operational costs.

Qualitative – metrics that measure soft benefits such as improved customer satisfaction or employee loyalty.

Sample governance metrics may include:

- Number of duplicate entries/data quality issues

- Number of data breaches/non-compliance issues

- Percent of returned mail due to incorrect addresses

- Level of accuracy for data field entries

- Percent of time data conforms to governance policies

- Percent of operational costs reduced post data governance launch

- Time spent on data entry

- Time spent on data cleansing

Maintaining the involvement of executive management and executive sponsors is crucial, as linking data governance success metrics to wider business advantages makes them tangible. Regularly review these metrics with the responsible data owners/stewards, the data governance steering committee, and the executive sponsors.

Step-by-step Data Governance Implementation Guide by Carlos Barroso

Developing a Data Governance Implementation Roadmap is important because it provides a clear definition of the scope and goals of the data governance program, which helps to ensure that everyone involved has a common understanding of what is being achieved.

A roadmap also helps to prioritize data governance initiatives and ensures that resources are being allocated to the most important initiatives first. This helps to ensure that the organization is getting the most value from its data governance investments. On top of that, it helps to align data governance

Step-by-step Data Governance Implementation Guide by Carlos Barroso

initiatives with the overall business objectives of the organization. This helps to ensure that the data governance program is serving the needs of the business and not just the needs of the IT department.

A roadmap provides stakeholders with a clear understanding of what to expect from the data governance program, and when they can expect it. This helps to manage expectations and ensure that stakeholders are not frustrated by unmet expectations. Tracking progress is the best way to manage expectations, and the roadmap provides a means of tracking progress against the data governance initiatives, which helps to identify any areas where additional resources or support may be needed.

Lastly, the roadmap provides a common language and a shared understanding of the data governance program, which helps to facilitate communication and collaboration between all stakeholders. The implementation of the roadmap is crucial for defining the scope and goals of the data governance program, prioritizing initiatives, aligning with business objectives, managing expectations, tracking progress, and facilitating communication and collaboration between stakeholders.

Let's then start working on the practical sessions and start creating the implementation roadmap, as part of the phase 2 of the Data Governance implementation framework.

Outlining the road ahead - Develop an action plan for the data governance program

Developing an action plan for the data governance program is important because it provides a structured approach to managing and protecting an organization's data assets. As such, you should always start by assessing the current state of data governance within the organization. This includes identifying current processes, systems, and data assets. You should also develop a clear understanding of the goals and objectives of the data governance program. This includes defining key metrics to measure the success of the program.

From there, you should start considering the scope of the program and the needed roles to run it. Define the roles and responsibilities of the data governance team, including stakeholders and decision-

Step-by-step Data Governance Implementation Guide by Carlos Barroso

makers. At the same time, start developing a data governance framework that outlines policies, procedures, and standards for data management and usage. This should include guidelines for data classification, privacy, security, and retention.

The program should also include the implementation of data management tools and systems to support the data governance program. This can include data catalogs, metadata repositories, and data quality tools. Along with those tools, designing and planning the delivery of training and resources to support the adoption of the data governance program across the organization is of equal importance. This includes providing guidance on data management best practices and policies.

As a last point in the plan, the transition to monitoring and evaluation of the effectiveness of the data governance program, including regular assessments of data quality and compliance with policies and procedures, will fully complement the plan and give certainty of a well-planned program implementation, promoting responsible data management and usage across the organization.

Data Governance Drivers

The drivers of your data governance project will directly influence the path you take. In fact, the drivers of a data governance project play a crucial role in determining the path the project takes. The drivers of a data governance project refer to the reasons or motivations for implementing data governance in an organization. Some common drivers for data governance include:

Step-by-step Data Governance Implementation Guide by Carlos Barroso

Compliance	Security	Availability	Trust
Select internal auditors to conduct semi-annual data audits.	Identify stakeholders, establish decision rights, and clarify accountabilities for access management.	Data owners play a critical role in data availability. Assign data owner roles to employees on the business side. Have the data owners take on the responsibility of granting permissions and access to the data.	Identify and implement data stewards. Establish their decision rights and clarify their accountabilities.
Establish processes to enforce regulatory, contractual, and architectural compliance requirements. Procure tools to protect data and manage policies.	Develop processes to align data governance with a security framework. Help assess risk and define controls to mitigate risk.	Conduct regular backup data audits and perform data archival tests. Mitigate the loss of data by establishing data backup policies.	Start to define escalation procedures for handling quality exceptions. To ensure quality and trust, develop a data cleansing process.
Look at adopting tokenization solutions and policy management software.	Look to procure tools to locate sensitive data, protect data, or manage policies or controls.	Deploy data backup tools and implement manual database failover.	Implement various solutions to maintain overall data quality. Leverage data cleansing and profiling tools to circumvent large data problems.
Focus governance efforts on data that is under regulatory scrutiny such as employee data that must be compliant with HIPAA or credit card data that must be PCI compliant.	Implement tokenization, data masking, and data vault solutions. Start with data that is most sensitive. The sensitivity of data directly affects the level of encryption required and the data security methods used.		Focus governance efforts towards reference data.

Checkpoint: Inventory current requirements and understand constraints

Ensure you are aware of the items listed below. If not, make a note to revisit them later. Requirements are not just obtained from interviews. Conduct an updated assessment of the following items:

Regulations the business must adhere to, including industry-specific regulations such as HIPAA, SEC, BASEL, and SOX, as well as regional regulations regarding data/records retention, tax laws, privacy laws, and data sovereignty laws.

- Policies and standards currently in place within the organization.
- Data governance processes that are currently in operation.
- Any current charters, such as an IT steering committee charter.
- The organization's IT strategic plans.
- Enterprise architecture frameworks.
- Organizational technology standards.
- Cloud policies in place.

Requirements can also take the form of constraints:

Step-by-step Data Governance Implementation Guide by Carlos Barroso

- System constraints, such as an inability to modify commercial application data models to improve data integrity (suggesting that certain technological processes cannot be employed).
- Consider budget limitations.
- Determine if any skills constraints exist within the organization to identify any necessary training requirements.
- The skills required for data quality analysis, compliance implementation, data security, and data integration should also be considered.

Generating Your Roadmap keeping in mind stakeholder buy-in

Implement the Data Governance program in a phased manner, starting with the most important data set.

Adopt a step-by-step approach to ensure that the established standards, procedures, and policies can be carried over to other data sets as the program progresses.

- One common mistake organizations make when planning for data governance is trying to fix all data issues across the entire organization at once, by first addressing the data set causing the biggest problems.

- Instead, it's more effective to start by focusing on a single data set, improving its quality through cleaning, establishing data standards, and enforcing policies and processes for data entry. After the governance of this data set is completed, review what worked and apply those processes to the next data set.

- By taking a phased approach to data governance, benefits and progress can be observed and measured at each stage. This approach also ensures continued support from executives and stakeholders, and can have a positive impact on the organization's bottom line.

Step-by-step Data Governance Implementation Guide by Carlos Barroso

Not all organizational data needs to be governed in the same way with the same policies and processes. Only the data set that supports the organization's most critical business operations requires the highest level of governance. Organizational data issues should be broken down into manageable phases. Attempting too much too soon will cause the governance initiative to fail.

Phase 3 - Implement and Drive the Data Governance Program

This phase focuses on putting the plans and initiatives developed in the previous phases into action and ensuring that the data governance program is properly implemented and effectively driving value for the organization. During this phase you will be deploying the data governance policies and procedures developed in the previous phases, and you will be communicating accordingly to all the stakeholders. You will establish the roles and responsibilities for data governance, and will be defining data quality standards as well as implementing data security and privacy policies.

Data governance technologies such as data catalogs, data dictionaries, and metadata management tools will now be implemented to support the data governance program, and this includes integrating these technologies with existing IT systems and processes.

This is also the phase for training and communication. All stakeholders should receive training on the data governance policies, procedures, and technologies, and regular communication should be established to ensure that everyone is aware of the data governance program and how it impacts them.

A very important aspect of this program is the monitoring and measurement, and this is also going to be implemented during this phase. Regular monitoring and measurement should be established to ensure that the data governance program is meeting its goals and delivering value to the organization. This includes regularly reviewing data quality, data security and privacy, and the effectiveness of the data governance policies and procedures.

And because nothing stays the same, in particular with today's fast moving economies, continuous improvement becomes also a key component of the implementation aspects of the Data Governance program. The data governance program should be continuously improved based on feedback from stakeholders and the results of the monitoring and measurement activities. This includes regularly reviewing and updating policies and procedures, and implementing new technologies and processes as needed.

In summary, Phase 3 of the Implementation of Data Governance focuses on putting the plans and initiatives developed in the previous phases into action and ensuring that the data governance program is effectively driving value for the organization. The key activities in this phase include deploying data governance policies and procedures, implementing data governance technologies, training and communication, monitoring and measurement, and continuous improvement.

Put the people and technology in position

When everyone involved in data governance understands their specific responsibilities, it becomes easier to address data-related issues and implement data-related initiatives in a timely and effective manner. Additionally, clearly defined roles and responsibilities reduce confusion and minimize the risk of duplication of efforts or missed opportunities. This, in turn, helps to ensure that data governance initiatives are aligned with the organization's overall objectives and that the organization is better positioned to make data-driven decisions.

Leverage technology platforms that can make your data governance program easier to track and enforce. Although you should not depend only on the software, technology is a must, in particular in today's fast moving corporate environments. Nevertheless, before looking at the technology, better to set up the entire framework. Only then start looking into potential technologies that could further enhance the program.

Step-by-step Data Governance Implementation Guide by Carlos Barroso

Implement a comprehensive data surveillance system to build trust in data utilization.

Utilize a data profile software solution to inspect data sets in batch mode and determine compliance with established rules for good data. The results of the inspection will be documented in reports and stored in a metadata repository for further analysis. A monitoring report should be created to provide a summary of the data's overall state. Ensure that the results are communicated clearly to all relevant stakeholders, promoting transparency and awareness of the data's quality and any areas for improvement. Establish a routine of generating monitoring reports on a daily, weekly, and monthly basis.

Establish a review process with data stewards. It's crucial to have a designated person, the data steward, in charge of fixing any errors that are reported by the data monitoring tools. Designate a person to manage and oversee the monitoring results. This individual should be responsible for scheduling regular meetings to assess the data errors and take action accordingly.

Identifying and addressing data defects early on can provide significant value and prevent them from becoming widespread problems.

Start executing the initiatives outlined in your roadmap and plan. As you progress through each step of the blueprint, construct your data governance implementation plan.

Documentation is essential. Keep records of the results of each activity in the Data Governance Implementation Plan Template, and you should have a nearly completed implementation plan by the end of the blueprint. This document will provide a clear outline of what is needed to effectively implement each task.

Upon completion, this document should be thoroughly reviewed and used to gain support and funding for implementation. It can also be utilized for training and standardizing data governance practices.

Customize the governance structure, roles and responsibilities, and policies and procedures to suit the size of your organization. In smaller organizations with limited personnel, responsibilities may need to be shared among staff instead of having dedicated full-time roles.

Step-by-step Data Governance Implementation Guide by Carlos Barroso

Assemble a cross-functional project team to address a range of business and IT needs. People are a crucial component of the data governance program. Identify key participants within your organization who are committed to making it a success.

Involving representatives from both IT and the business will provide diverse perspectives and contribute to a well-rounded and comprehensive data governance vision. The data governance team will play a crucial role in driving the success of the project by making important decisions such as evaluating business needs, selecting and prioritizing solutions, and communicating initiatives.

The size of the team should be optimal, allowing for efficient decision-making while also comprising representatives from both business and IT units. The composition of the team may vary depending on the resources available within the organization, but could include key members such as:

- **Chief Data Officer (CDO)** – a senior business executive who supervises data stewardship and policy.
- **Data Steward** – a champion business person accountable for data quality in their particular area.
- **Subject Matter Experts** – business analysts who have a firm understanding of the critical processes and systems, and enough knowledge of the data to identify errors and set standards.
- **IT Director / Manager** – a senior employee who maintains information technology strategies through data research and analysis, implements technical strategic solutions, and manages staff.
- **Data Owner** – an employee who is accountable for the integrity, quality, and security of a specific domain of data.
- **Database Administrators or System Analysts** – employees who oversee the performance of the database and take responsibility for the quality and integrity of the data.

Securing support and involvement from key players within the organization is crucial for the success of the data governance initiative. Identify and engage business leaders and data owners, who are heavily impacted by data governance issues, as early champions of the project.

Step-by-step Data Governance Implementation Guide by Carlos Barroso

Incorporating the role of a Chief Data Officer (CDO) can provide a top-down approach to establishing the necessary management rigor for the organization's data assets. This executive-level position can drive the data governance agenda forward and ensure its importance is recognized throughout the organization.

Enable the CDO to exercise executive authority.

Assign adequate authority to the CDO to ensure their effectiveness in managing data initiatives. Adequate resources should also be made available to the CDO to successfully execute projects and achieve data management goals.

Ensure the appropriate skill set.

The CDO must have a combination of technical abilities and business and interpersonal skills to overcome any technical and political obstacles that may arise during the implementation of data governance.

Create defined responsibilities.

To ensure the success of the CDO role, it is essential to establish clear goals and objectives that align with the business. This will ensure that the relatively new position of CDO is able to effectively drive data governance initiatives.

Ensure Executive Support for Data Governance. The CDO's crucial role is to promote the significance of data governance and take a top-down approach in doing so. By effectively communicating the importance of data governance, the common challenges in obtaining funding and resources for the program can be minimized.

Make sure you have committees that span across strategic, tactical, and operational duties.

There is no one-size-fits-all data governance structure. However, most organizations follow a similar pattern when establishing committees, councils, and cross-functional groups. They strive to identify roles and responsibilities at a **strategic**, **tactical**, and **operational** level. Factors such as the focus of the data governance project and the maturity and size of the organization will influence the structure of the program.

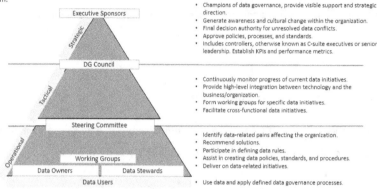

- Champions of data governance, provide visible support and strategic direction.
- Generate awareness and cultural change within the organization.
- Final decision authority for unresolved data conflicts.
- Approve policies, processes, and standards.
- Includes controllers, otherwise known as C-suite executives or senior leadership. Establish KPIs and performance metrics.

- Continuously monitor progress of current data initiatives.
- Provide high-level integration between technology and the business/organization.
- Form working groups for specific data initiatives.
- Facilitate cross-functional data initiatives.

- Identify data-related pains affecting the organization.
- Recommend solutions.
- Participate in defining data rules.
- Assist in creating data policies, standards, and procedures.
- Deliver on data-related initiatives.

- Use data and apply defined data governance processes.

Data Governance Council:

Generally:
- Senior executive representatives operating at the organization's strategic level.
- Aligns business strategies and goals to data strategies and data management plans.
- Supports top-down approach to DG and helps to socialize DG/DM and support adoption.

Data Governance Steering Committee:

Generally:
- Cross-functional body responsible for creating tactical plans related to data governance.
- Manages data- and practice-related issues.
- Monitors and guides data governance/data management initiatives.
- Oversees performance and management of working groups.

Data Stewards:

Traditionally, data stewards:
- Serve on an operational level addressing issues related to adherence to standards/procedures, monitoring data quality, raising issues identified, etc.
- Are responsible for managing access, quality, escalating issues, etc.

Data Owners:

Traditionally, data owners:
- Are ultimately accountable for all issues related to the data assets under their purview.
- Are business leaders with team members who are heavy users of the data assets.
- **Review** the **permissions** of user groups to different data sets.
- **Assess** the **quality of the data** and whether it enables employees to perform their jobs efficiently.
- **Determine the business impact** of changing permission statuses.
- Understand the lifecycle of the data.

Data Governance Working Groups:

Working groups are the cross-functional teams that deliver on data governance projects, initiatives, and ad hoc review committees.

Establish a Data Governance Council to be the final authority in the Data Governance program. This council will be responsible for overseeing the usage, generation, and maintenance of data. The size of the council may vary depending on the organization, with larger organizations requiring a larger group of individuals. To ensure effective governance, it is recommended to include an executive sponsor as a member of the council.

The responsibilities of the data governance council include guiding the direction for future data initiatives, establishing guidelines for new policies and procedures, and authorizing changes to existing ones. They also resolve issues raised by the steering committee. The council should consist of top

Step-by-step Data Governance Implementation Guide by Carlos Barroso

executives such as the CEO, CIO, CFO, CDO, and other senior management, to help secure their commitment to data-related initiatives.

The steering committee, consisting of both business and IT representatives, will drive the governance project. They must have a comprehensive understanding of both the organization's data needs and the limitations of the current IT infrastructure and applications. With the necessary political authority, the steering committee is responsible for making decisions on how data is managed, its contents, and retention according to regulatory requirements. They serve as the governing body and final decision-makers for data processes, policies, and standards throughout the organization.

An effective steering committee should have a team size of five to ten individuals, depending on the size and complexity of the organization. The team should be large enough to represent key stakeholders but small enough to be able to carry out tasks efficiently.

Core Goals of a Data Governance Steering Committee

Bridge the gap between the data governance council and working groups to enhance data-driven decision-making.

- Guarantee that information is unambiguously defined and widely understood.
- Establish trustworthy data as a valuable corporate asset.
- Enhance the uniformity of data usage across the enterprise.

The Steering Committee should include representation from the following four groups of key stakeholders:

- Data Owners
- Business Subject Matter Experts

Step-by-step Data Governance Implementation Guide by Carlos Barroso

- Business Process Owners
- Data Stewards.

Summary of the Data Governance Implementation

A comprehensive Data Governance Implementation plan in an organization involves several key elements to ensure its success. To start with, the organization must grant the right level of authority to its CDO, who is responsible for managing data initiatives and must have the necessary resources to carry out projects effectively. The CDO should have both technical and business skills, as well as people skills to tackle the technical and political challenges of data governance.

It's also crucial for the organization to establish complete C-suite buy-in by having the CDO act as a data governance evangelist. To this end, the organization can create a data governance council, which serves as the ultimate authority in data governance programs. This council, consisting of executives and representatives from both business and IT, must set clear outcomes and objectives and should be given the political authority to make decisions on data-related policies, processes, and standards.

The organization's steering committee, which drives the governance project, must comprise business and IT representatives who understand the data needs of the business and the technological limitations of the IT infrastructure. The steering committee must act as the governing body and final voice regarding organizational data processes, policies, and standards and authorize any changes before implementation.

The data governance steering committee's core objectives are to improve data-driven decisions, ensure consistent data definition and understanding, establish trusted data as an enterprise asset, and improve the consistency of data use across the organization. The steering committee should comprise four categories of key stakeholders: data owners, business subject matter experts, business process owners, and data stewards.

Step-by-step Data Governance Implementation Guide by Carlos Barroso

In conclusion, a well-executed Data Governance Implementation plan involves granting the right level of authority to the CDO, establishing complete C-suite buy-in, creating a data governance council and steering committee, and setting clear objectives and responsibilities.